BR STEAM IN THE NORTH OF ENGLAND

JOHN WHITELEY

AMBERLEY

First published 2023

Amberley Publishing
The Hill, Stroud
Gloucestershire, GL5 4EP

www.amberley-books.com

Copyright © John Whiteley, 2023

ISBN 978 1 3981 1644 3 (print)
ISBN 978 1 3981 1645 0 (ebook)

British Library Cataloguing in Publication Data.
A catalogue record for this book is available from
the British Library.

Origination by Amberley Publishing.
Printed in the UK.

Introduction

Having been born at Halifax and then living only a few miles away at Lightcliffe where I attended junior school, it is not surprising that my first memories of railways were very much in that area. While at junior school I remember being fascinated by L&YR 0-6-0s shunting the goods yard, and later some of my first photographs were taken there when I was about thirteen, using the inevitable Brownie 127 camera, but unfortunately neither the prints nor the negatives have survived.

In my early teens I did relatively little trainspotting, although I did sometimes cycle to Brighouse to see the 'half twelver', which was almost guaranteed to produce a namer, generally either *Mars* or *Dauntless* of Bank Hall, on the Liverpool–Newcastle express. A longer cycle ride took me to Heaton Lodge Junction at Mirfield, an extremely busy spot with not only all the Calder Valley traffic, but also the more glamorous Standedge line expresses producing Royal Scots and the like.

A few years later, when I was at grammar school at Cleckheaton, I developed a keen interest in photography, and my recently acquired Yashica fixed lens 35 mm camera was soon pointed at steam locomotives. I also started to do my own processing, and after developing the black and white film, I couldn't wait to get into my improvised darkroom, and still recall the thrill of the image appearing in the developer. How different it is these days with modern digital technology and cameras producing instant pictures. However, it is now possible to scan those early negatives, and with the help of Photoshop a better image can often be obtained from a tricky negative than a wet print would ever produce.

In those early days of my railway photography, Leeds could easily be reached by bus from my home at Lightcliffe, and the small, rather scruffy terminus at Leeds Central was one of my favourite stations. With the aid of a line-side photographic permit that I had obtained, I was able to take many pictures there of the magnificent LNER Pacifics, and also on the steep climb from Central station to Copley Hill. At the larger Leeds City station a variety of both LNER and LMS power could be seen and the highlight of the day in the early afternoon at the Wellington side of Leeds City was the arrival of both the 'Thames-Clyde Express' and the 'Waverley', both trains reversing there and changing locomotives.

Not having my own transport at that time I often had to rely on hitchhiking to get further afield to the likes of Shap, Carlisle, and sometimes even further north to Scotland. However, things changed towards the end of 1962 after I had started working in an architects and surveyors office in Dewsbury, when I bought a second-hand Vespa scooter. This enabled travel to more inaccessible locations, but sadly I tended to ignore interesting lines on my own doorstep, which were in danger of either imminent closure or dieselisation. With the benefit of hindsight I would have no doubt approached my railway photography somewhat differently at that time.

However, the considerable time I spent alone on the desolate Westmorland Fells was a pure delight. Interspersed with the wild cry of the curlew, the sight and sound of a Duchess storming up from Tebay on an Anglo-Scottish express, or a heavy freight with banking assistance struggling towards Shap Summit, will stay with me forever.

Delving through my own collection of pictures in the preparation of this book, augmented by a few from my collection, has been a real pleasure, reminding me of times past. Not only has the lure of steam been such an important part of my life, but it has also resulted in many cherished lifelong friendships with kindred spirits.

With sanders on, Peppercorn class A1 Pacific No. 60158 *Aberdonian* leaves York with an express for Newcastle on Good Friday 31 March 1961. Built in 1949, *Aberdonian* was initially shedded at Kings Cross, but moved several times before arriving at Doncaster in 1958, from where it was withdrawn towards the end of 1964.

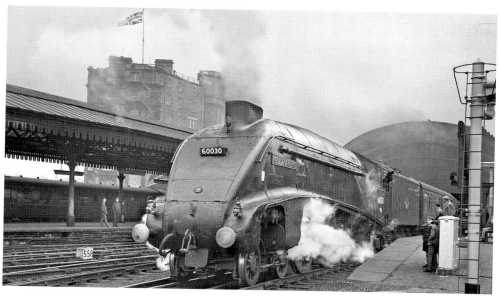

The north end of platform 9 at York was a popular position for spotters, and several are watching Kings Cross class A4 Pacific No. 60030 *Golden Fleece* leaving with an express from Kings Cross to Edinburgh on 31 March 1961. Originally named *Great Snipe* when it was built in 1937, it was almost immediately renamed *Golden Fleece* when it was selected for use on the LNER 'West Riding Limited' streamlined train, which ran between Kings Cross, Leeds and Bradford. In 1951 it was fitted with a corridor tender, which it retained until withdrawal at the end of 1962, enabling non-stop running between Kings Cross and Edinburgh.

At the south end of platform 9 on 28 April 1962 Gresley class V2 2-6-2 No. 60918 prepares to leave with the 10.21 a.m. York–Bournemouth formed of SR stock. No. 60918 was built in 1941 and spent its entire life shedded at York until withdrawal in October 1962.

Kings Cross A4 Pacific No. 60013 *Dominion of New Zealand* is accelerating the 9.40 a.m. Glasgow–Kings Cross express away from its stop at York on 1 September 1962. In 1939 *Dominion of New Zealand* had been fitted with a New Zealand Government Railways whistle, which was larger and pitched lower in sound than the standard A4 chime whistle.

On 2 May 1964 inside the roundhouse at York, now part of the National Railway Museum. Peppercorn class A1 Pacifics No. 60150 *Willbrook* and No. 60121 *Silurian* are on their home shed and are flanked by Ivatt class 4 2-6-0 No. 43078 of Hull Dairycoates on the left and Gresley class V2 2-6-2 No. 60929 of Gateshead on the right.

A view of the shed yard at York taken from the coaling tower on 19 October 1963, by which time diesels had already started to arrive. On the left is Peppercorn class K1 2-6-0 No. 62062, which had recently been transferred to York from Darlington. Gresley A4 Pacific No. 60019 *Bittern* is visiting from Gateshead and is facing Thompson class B1 4-6-0 No. 61031 *Reedbuck*, which is also on its home shed and partly obscuring a visiting class O4 2-8-0.

Running alongside the River Ouse and with 50A York motive power depot out of sight on the left, Peppercorn class A1 Pacific No. 60121 *Silurian* is nearing the station with an Up parcels and empty stock train on 19 October 1963. *Silurian* was built in 1948, named in 1950 after a horse that won the 1923 Doncaster Cup, and spent its entire life shedded at York until withdrawal towards the end of 1965.

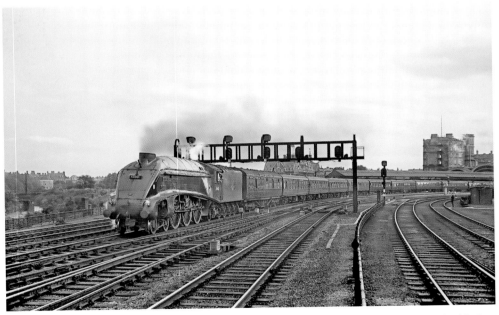

Gresley class A4 Pacific No. 60001 *Sir Ronald Matthews* spent its entire life shedded at Gateshead and is curving away from York station heading a Kings Cross–Newcastle express on Saturday 1 September 1962. In the background is the prestigious Royal Station Hotel.

On Good Friday 31 March 1961, after a walk of almost 2 miles from York station, Gresley class A3 Pacific No. 60086 *Gainsborough* of Leeds Neville Hill is nearing Skelton Junction with a Liverpool–Newcastle express, which it has taken over from LMS power at Leeds City.

Shortly after *Gainsborough* had passed heading north on 31 March 1961, Thompson class A2/3 Pacific No. 60514 *Chamossaire* of New England came south heading an Up Bank Holiday extra. It is passing Skelton Junction signal box and slowing for Severus Curve at Clifton before arriving at York station. Only fifteen class A2/3s were built at Doncaster shortly before nationalisation and the majority of the class were allocated to the North Eastern area, although *Chamossaire* was initially allocated to Kings Cross but soon moved to New England from where it was withdrawn in December 1962.

On Saturday 24 June 1961 I spent a few hours in the afternoon on the West Coast main line near Hartford, about 4 miles south of Weaver Junction, not knowing that the electrification for the Liverpool services was already in place, but not yet switched on. Stanier Princess Royal Pacific No. 46200 *The Princess Royal* of Crewe North is heading south with the 10.15 a.m. Glasgow–Euston.

Towards the end of the afternoon Carlisle Upperby Princess Coronation Pacific No. 46250 *City of Lichfield* came north heading a Down express. By the look of the exhaust all was not well on the footplate of this Duchess, as the Coronation Pacifics were generally known.

Having been taken on holiday to Morecambe by my parents in the summer of 1959, I soon found my way to nearby Hest Bank on the West Coast main line, which was a mecca for trainspotters. These two youngsters are watching a southbound express restarting from the station headed by Newton Heath Jubilee 4-6-0 No. 45701 *Conqueror* and a Britannia Pacific.

Later on the same day in early August 1959, one of the attractive Fowler parallel boiler Patriot 4-6-0s No. 45501 *St Dunstan's* of Crewe North is rushing north towards Hest Bank station past the customary group of spotters.

Having travelled by train to Chester on summer bank holiday Monday 7 August 1961, I then walked the 2 miles or so to Saltney Junction where the North Wales line and the GWR line to Wrexham part. One of the first trains I saw was the 11.55 a.m. Manchester Exchange–Llandudno and Holyhead on the North Wales line hauled by Willesden Britannia Pacific No. 70033 *Charles Dickens*.

Early in the afternoon of 7 August 1961, Castle class 4-6-0 No. 5046 *Earl Cawdor* of Wolverhampton Stafford Road is accelerating away from the junction on the GWR line heading the 9.10 a.m. Paddington–Birkenhead.

Also on 7 August 1961, Stafford Road Castle No. 5019 *Treago Castle* has just passed the racecourse and is accelerating towards Saltney Junction heading empty coaching stock, probably for Shrewsbury.

Seen from Chester No. 6 signal box on Saturday 30 May 1964, Worcester Grange class 4-6-0 No. 6806 *Blackwell Grange* is curving away from Chester General with the 11.40 a.m. Birkenhead–Paddington, which presumably it will take as far as Shrewsbury. It was surprising to see a Worcester engine at Chester and during the 1950s *Blackwell Grange* had spent spells at Penzance, Chester, Hereford and Oxley before moving to Worcester in June 1961, from where it was withdrawn in November 1964.

Overlooked by the signal box that controlled the west end of Chester General station, Shrewsbury Jubilee class 4-6-0 No. 45699 *Galatea*, which is now fortunately preserved, is leaving with an afternoon Birkenhead–Paddington express on 30 May 1964.

Stanier Pacifics were not uncommon at Chester General, and on 30 May 1964 Crewe North Duchess No. 46254 *City of Stoke-on-Trent* arrived with the afternoon parcels from Holyhead to Crewe. After getting some photographs of it pausing at the station, a hasty trackside departure was made in order to get it climbing away from the station past the motive power depot on its way to Crewe.

Among my earliest memories of railways was when I was about six or seven years old when I was often taken by my parents to Shibden Park near Halifax from home at Lightcliffe. Adjacent to the playground the line from Halifax to Bradford could be seen emerging from Beacon Hill Tunnel shortly after leaving Halifax. At this location several years later, Bank Hall Jubilee class 4-6-0 No. 45717 *Dauntless* is heading a Liverpool–Bradford Exchange train. It was probably taken in spring 1959, when as a youngster I was using a cheap camera that struggled to stop anything moving quickly.

On Saturday 10 September 1966, just round the corner from Beacon Hill Tunnel, one of the last Jubilees to remain in service, No. 45565, formerly named *Victoria*, but with the nameplates removed, is heading the summer Saturday 1.25 p.m. Bridlington–Bradford Exchange. *Victoria* had spent many years at Leeds Holbeck, but in June 1965 it was moved to Low Moor, from where it was withdrawn in January 1967.

The summer Saturday Bridlington–Bradford Exchange is leaving platform 3 at Halifax alongside Halifax East signal box in September 1966, surprisingly headed by Carlisle Kingmoor Black Five 4-6-0 No. 45295.

The line between Thornhill LNW Junction and Heaton Lodge Junction was particularly busy, at one time operated jointly by the L&YR and the L&NWR. Among other things, there was a constant flow of coal traffic between Yorkshire and Lancashire, some using the Calder Valley route and some the more difficult route over Standedge. This westbound coal train appears to be taking the Standedge route via Huddersfield and is nearing Mirfield on 13 April 1964 hauled by a typically scruffy Wakefield class WD 2-8-0 No. 90721.

Jubilee class 4-6-0 No. 45623 *Palestine* of Crewe South is accelerating a lengthy mixed freight from Lancashire for Leeds away from a signal check near Mirfield on Saturday 16 September 1961.

Mirfield WD class 2-8-0 No. 90068 is passing Thornhill LNW Junction signal box on 13 March 1963 with a rake of coal empties for Healey Mills. At Thornhill LNW Junction the line to Dewsbury and Leeds curved away from the Wakefield line and the box was elevated to enable sighting over the adjacent road bridge.

Also taken at Thornhill LNW Junction on Wednesday 13 March 1963 during my lunch hour while working nearby in Dewsbury, WD class 2-8-0 No. 90692 is heading a westbound mixed freight while in the distance another WD is heading a westbound coal train. The Leeds line is curving off to the left adjacent to Thornhill Power Station, with Ravensthorpe station obscured by the exhaust.

It seems like another lunchtime, this time on Monday 15 October 1962, was spent at the line-side, this time at Thornhill Junction where the line from Low Moor joins the Calder Valley main line. Black Five No. 44735 of Newton Heath is coasting past with a mixed freight of empties heading for Healey Mills, presumably from the Manchester area. The Spen Valley line to Low Moor can be seen curving away to the right.

Jubilee class 4-6-0 No. 45565 *Victoria* had moved from Leeds Holbeck to Low Moor in June 1962 when diesels were starting to replace steam on some of the passenger turns at Holbeck. Now relegated to working coal empties from Low Moor to Healey Mills, on 15 October 1962 it is restarting its train at Thornhill Junction having had to wait at the signal for the road on to the main line.

It appears that Wakefield WD 2-8-0 No. 90604 has recently had a works visit, and on Monday 15 October 1962 it is passing the remains of Thornhill station, which had closed to passengers in January 1962. It will shortly be turning right at Thornhill Junction with an engineer's train from Healey Mills to Low Moor.

An unusual visitor passing through Wakefield Kirkgate on Sunday 13 May 1962. SR Schools class 4-4-0 No. 30925 *Cheltenham* is piloting LMS class 2P 4-4-0 No. 40646 on the RCTS 'East Midlander No. 5' rail tour from Nottingham Victoria to Darlington. *Cheltenham* was shedded at Basingstoke at the time, but was temporarily moved to Annesley for the special and the 2P had been borrowed from Bescot.

On Saturday 26 May 1962 Rose Grove WD 2-8-0 No. 90295 is drifting past Brighouse with a rake of coal empties from Lancashire to Healey Mills.

A slightly unusual sight in the Calder Valley on 26 May 1962 was a class 01 2-8-0 No. 63571, which had been rebuilt by Thompson with a new round-topped boiler from a Robinson GCR class 04. No. 63571 was shedded at Staveley GC and is taking water in the extensive yard at Brighouse heading a Saturday coal train from the Midlands to the recently opened Elland Power Station.

After taking water in the yard at Brighouse, No. 63571 is accelerating its westbound coal train past Brighouse station on the easy grade up the Calder Valley towards nearby Elland.

On 23 April 1961 Bank Hall unrebuilt Patriot 4-6-0 No. 45517 is accelerating away from its stop at Mirfield on the shortened Sunday 10.30 a.m. Liverpool Exchange–Newcastle, which took the Calder Valley route, unlike the Liverpool Lime Street–Newcastle expresses that took the Standedge route. No. 45517 had moved from Willesden to Bank Hall in July 1958 and was a regular performer on this train until withdrawal in June 1962.

Normanton class 4F 0-6-0 No. 44408 struggles to restart a freight of mainly coal from Healey Mills to Low Moor, having been stopped at Heckmondwike Junction on 14 March 1963. It has just passed beneath the New Line built by the L&NWR around 1900, which ran from Heaton Lodge Junction at Mirfield, providing direct access to Leeds New (later Leeds City). The line diverging to the right is the little used L&YR connection to Mirfield.

The Leeds portion of the 2.20 p.m. Manchester Victoria–Bradford and Leeds has been detached at Low Moor and is seen shortly after leaving on Sunday 24 September 1961 behind Fairburn class 4 2-6-4T No. 42151.

For several Sundays in September and October 1961 the line between Leeds and Wakefield Westgate was closed due to major engineering work resulting in trains being diverted via Hare Park Junction, Wakefield Kirkgate and Thornhill Junction to Low Moor where the Bradford and Leeds portions were separated. On 24 September Kings Cross A4 Pacific No. 60003 *Andrew K. McCosh* has just left Low Moor with the Bradford portion of the 10.25 a.m. Kings Cross–Leeds and Bradford. The Leeds portion left shortly afterwards behind a Black Five travelling via the avoiding line from Bowling Junction to Laisterdyke and on to Leeds Central.

On 24 September 1961 Copley Hill A1 Pacific No. 60133 *Pommern* is about to leave Low Moor with the diverted 4.38 p.m. Leeds–Kings Cross. It had brought the portion from Bradford Exchange and just combined with the main Leeds portion, which had arrived earlier behind a Black Five as the large LNER Pacifics were not allowed to use the avoiding line between Bowling Junction and Laisterdyke.

On Sunday 8 October 1961 Kings Cross A4 Pacific No. 60032 *Gannet* is accelerating away from a speed restriction at Cleckheaton Central towards Heckmondwike with the diverted 12.45 p.m. Leeds Central–Kings Cross, which had combined with the Bradford portion at Low Moor. This is now part of the 7-mile-long Spen Valley Greenway cycle and footpath, which was formed after the line was closed.

Several local spotters are watching Gresley class A3 Pacific No. 60044 *Melton* of Kings Cross passing Cleckheaton Central with the diverted 10.25 a.m. Kings Cross–Leeds and Bradford on 8 October 1961. Built by the L&YR, Cleckheaton Central closed to passenger traffic in 1965 and to freight about four years later and part of this site is now a supermarket and car park.

Saturday 6 January 1962 was a bright, frosty day in Lancashire and two southbound freights are climbing away from Preston near Leyland. On the right Lostock Hall WD 2-8-0 No. 90675 will take the Bolton and Manchester line at nearby Euxton Junction and on the left a Hughes/Fowler Crab 2-6-0 will continue south on the West Coast main line towards Wigan.

Glinting in the low winter sun on 6 January 1962, the 13.30 Manchester Victoria–Carlisle express has just passed Euxton Junction with recently ex-works Black Five No. 44942 of Aston, which is possibly on a running in turn, piloting Royal Scot 4-6-0 No. 46142 *The York & Lancaster Regiment* of Newton Heath.

Caprotti fitted Black Five 4-6-0 No. 44742 of Bank Hall is accelerating away from Leyland on 6 January 1962 with a stopping train, thought to be from Blackpool to Manchester.

Towards the end of BR steam numerous rail tours were run, and on Thursday 18 May 1968 the last surviving Pacific, Britannia No. 70013 *Oliver Cromwell*, is leaving Preston on a section of line which no longer exists and is now car parking. With several enthusiasts trackside, it is heading the 'North Western Steam Tour' organised by the Warwickshire Railway Society. Several locomotives were used on the tour and *Oliver Cromwell* worked from Preston to Morecambe via Blackburn and Hellifield.

One of the last regular BR steam turns was a parcels train to Barrow from Preston, and on Thursday 27 July 1968 Black Five No. 45025 is leaving Carnforth and has just passed Carnforth F&M Junction signal box on a morning Preston–Barrow parcels. Its shed code of 10A Carnforth can be seen on the smokebox door, and it was withdrawn from there only a few days later.

I spent many happy hours on the station at Carlisle Citadel, and on Tuesday 28 July 1964, with the station clock showing 12.10 p.m., Kingmoor Duchess Pacific No. 46255 *City of Hereford* is preparing to leave on the 10.05 a.m. Glasgow–Birmingham, having just been checked by the wheel tapper.

Royal Scot 4-6-0 No. 46118 *Royal Welch Fusilier* of Carlisle Upperby is curving away from the platform at Carlisle heading the 9.30 a.m. Manchester–Glasgow on Easter Sunday 29 March 1964.

By August 1964 all five remaining BR Standard Clan Pacifics were shedded at Carlisle Kingmoor, the five that had been at Polmadie having been withdrawn at the end of 1962 by the Scottish Region in their efforts to eliminate express steam locomotives as quickly as possible. No. 72007 *Clan Mackintosh* has just passed its home shed with the 9.25 a.m. Crewe–Perth and Aberdeen on Monday 10 August 1964.

On Saturday 23 April 1966 the Altrinchamian Railway Enthusiasts Society ran the 'Waverley Special' from Manchester Exchange to Edinburgh hauled by Peppercorn class A2 Pacific No. 60528 *Tudor Minstrel* of Dundee. I photographed it climbing Shap in driving rain, but by Carlisle the weather was starting to clear and shortly after leaving Carlisle it is near Longtown on the lower reaches of the Waverley route to Edinburgh.

The 8.15 a.m. Up parcels to Crewe has just left Carlisle on Monday 10 August 1964 and is climbing the short section of 1 in 110 hauled by Upperby rebuilt Patriot 4-6-0 No. 45527 *Southport*. Diverging to the right is the line to Petteril Bridge Junction where the Settle and Carlisle and Newcastle routes separate.

Scruffy Warrington Jubilee 4-6-0 No. 45583 *Assam* is making a vigorous departure from Carlisle on Monday 10 August 1964, heading home with the 7.11 p.m. to Warrington. It has recently been applied with diagonal yellow stripes on the cab sides denoting it being restricted from working south of Crewe under the energised 25 kv catenary, but would only have another few weeks in service before being withdrawn.

My first of subsequently numerous visits to Shap was over the spring bank holiday weekend of 1961. Having hitchhiked from home in the West Riding to Penrith, I then set off walking south on the lineside towards my intended camp site near Little Strickland. The southbound climb to Shap Summit starts in earnest just south of Penrith, but with a gradient generally of about 1 in 125 it is not as steep as the northbound climb to the summit. On Sunday 21 May 1961 Polmadie Royal Scot No. 46107 *Argyll and Sutherland Highlander* has just passed Penrith heading the 11.00 a.m. Glasgow–Manchester.

Spring bank holiday 1962 was also spent on Shap, and on Saturday 9 June Jubilee class 4-6-0 No. 45703 *Thunderer* of Carlisle Upperby is coming round the sharp curve at Penrith heading an Up express freight. It has just passed Penrith No. 2 signal box where the line to Keswick and Workington leaves the main line.

Edge Hill Duchesses were not regularly seen on Shap, but on Saturday 25 July 1964 rather scruffy No. 46241 *City of Edinburgh* is climbing past the loop at Clifton & Lowther on the thirteen-coach 9.00 a.m. Perth–Euston.

No. 46233 *Duchess of Sutherland* was also shedded at Edge Hill when this photograph was taken on Easter Saturday 13 April 1963. It is heading an Up perishables freight including six loaded cattle wagons at the front, and is almost 2 miles south of Penrith, having just crossed the River Lowther. Towards the front of the train the M6 motorway now passes beneath the railway line.

Having photographed *Duchess of Sutherland* approaching Clifton & Lowther on 13 April 1963, I couldn't resist trying to get another photograph of it, so set off in chase on my trusty Vespa scooter. I think it must have been looped at Clifton & Lowther as I managed to get it again with several minutes to spare near Little Strickland, just north of Thrimby Grange.

On Sunday 10 June 1962, having camped overnight directly adjacent to the line just north of Little Strickland, I was waiting for the Up 'Royal Scot' at Bessygill expecting it to be diesel-hauled, but in the distance heard the unmistakable sound of a Duchess working hard. Round the corner appeared No. 46252 *City of Leicester* of Carlisle Kingmoor heading fourteen coaches. What I found out later was the Up 'Royal Scot' combined with the bank holiday relief due to the last minute failure of the booked diesel on the main train, *City of Leicester*, having been booked to work the relief.

On Easter Monday 30 March 1964 rebuilt Patriot 4-6-0 No. 45512 *Bunsen* of Carlisle Upperby is storming past the loop at Thrimby Grange on the unbroken 8-mile 1 in 125 climb from just south of Penrith. It is heading the bank holiday relief to the Up 'Royal Scot' and is passing where the M6 motorway now crosses the line.

After a very early start from home on Friday 21 August 1964 on my Vespa scooter to photograph A4s in Scotland, as I was crossing the line at Thrimby Grange I noticed in the distance the exhaust trail of a southbound train. A few minutes later Stanier class 6P5F 2-6-0 No. 42959 appeared alongside the River Leith on a mixed freight.

Long-time Bank Hall Jubilee No. 45698 *Mars*, now with yellow cab side stripe, is heading the 2.00 p.m. Glasgow–Manchester and Liverpool just north of Thrimby Grange near Little Strickland on Saturday 17 July 1965. By this time there were very few regular turns for ex-LMS passenger engines on the West Coast main line on express passenger trains, and on the right-hand side of the picture in the trees is where I had camped on several occasions a few years earlier.

The slightly scruffy and cramped terminus at Leeds Central with its eight platforms was among my favourite stations, but it sadly closed in May 1967 and the site subsequently redeveloped several times. On Tuesday 5 March 1963 the 9.42 a.m. express to Kings Cross is leaving behind Peppercorn class A1 Pacific No. 60133 *Pommern*, a long-term resident of Copley Hill shed at Leeds. Leeds Central 'A' box is on the right, which controlled the station area, and *Pommern* is just starting the gruelling, almost unbroken steep climb of about 6 miles to Ardsley.

The curvature of the track disguises the length of the 9.42 a.m. Leeds Central–Kings Cross express as it climbs away from the terminus past Leeds Central 'B' box, which controlled the line into the high level goods depot on the left. The express is headed by A1 Pacific No. 60148 *Aboyeur* of Copley Hill and is seen on Tuesday 14 May 1963.

On Saturday 3 February 1962 another of Copley Hill's stud of A1 Pacifics, No. 60120 *Kittiwake,* is climbing the 1 in 100 from Leeds Central with the Up 'Yorkshire Pullman' near Holbeck High Level station, which had closed in 1957. The line diverging to the left was the connection to Geldard Junction and the lines to Harrogate and Skipton. Part of this section of truncated viaduct still exists.

The Sunday 5.00 p.m. express to Kings Cross was a heavy train, and on 1 April 1962 has just left Leeds Central behind Kings Cross A4 Pacific No. 60029 *Woodcock*, which is slipping badly on the steep gradient. The line diverging to the left is to the high level goods depot.

On Sunday 1 July 1962 the heavy 4.40 p.m. express to Kings Cross is climbing past Holbeck Junction behind Copley Hill A1 No. 60117 *Bois Roussel*, having just passed the remains of Holbeck High Level station.

Gresley class A3 Pacific No. 60061 *Pretty Polly* of Kings Cross, fitted with trough smoke
deflectors in 1961, has just passed Holbeck Junction on 28 May 1963 with the Up 'White Rose'
to Kings Cross. The lines on the far left are to Bradford Exchange and in the foreground lead
into Copley Hill shed. At lower level on the right are the ex-L&NWR Copley Hill yards and the
Huddersfield line.

Another of Copley Hill's A1 Pacifics, No. 60145 *Saint Mungo,* is near the top of the climb from
Leeds Central, approaching Wortley South Junction, with Copley Hill shed on the left-hand side
partly obscured by the exhaust. It is heading a morning express to Kings Cross and was the last
Peppercorn A1 Pacific to be withdrawn in June 1966. The photograph was taken on Tuesday
19 March 1963, and at the time I was given half-day release from work to study at college for
my professional exams, but often photography around Leeds seemed a better option.

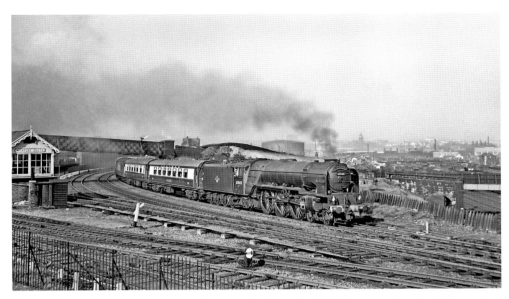

No. 60148 *Aboyeur* is seen again, this time hauling the Up 'Harrogate Sunday Pullman' on 16 April 1961. It has just passed Copley Hill shed at Wortley South Junction at the top of the climb from Leeds Central and is just about to have a short breather before continuing the climb to Ardsley. The lines on the left provided a direct route between Bradford Exchange and Doncaster avoiding Leeds Central, but closed in the early 1980s.

Gresley class A3 Pacific No. 60062 *Minoru* of Kings Cross is on the short downhill section having just passed Wortley South Junction with the Up 'Yorkshire Pullman' on Saturday 20 May 1961. It was to be fitted with trough smoke deflectors in July 1961 and was withdrawn in December 1964.

A view of Leeds Central taken from 'A' box on Saturday 25 April 1964 when many of the main line expresses were being taken over by diesels. Copley Hill A1 Pacific No. 60117 *Bois Roussel* was deputising for a Deltic, which was running very late on the Up 'Queen of Scots' from Edinburgh and was rostered to take the 5.10 p.m. to Kings Cross from Leeds, so *Bois Roussel* is preparing to leave in place of the Deltic. Its regular main line duties were almost at an end by this time, and it was finally withdrawn from Ardsley in January 1965.

On Saturday 17 June 1961 Kings Cross A4 Pacific No. 60028 *Walter K. Whigham* is speeding south near Heck heading the 9.45 a.m. Edinburgh Waverley–Kings Cross with the 'Elizabethan' headboard reversed. Eggborough Power Station would later be built on land to the left and Drax Power Station on land to the right.

Later in the day on 17 June 1961 Gresley V2 2-6-2 No. 60878 of York has just passed Heck heading the Down 'Scarborough Flyer'. The M62 motorway now crosses the East Coast main line at this spot.

The 9.45 a.m. Yarmouth–York has just sped past the small signal box at Heck behind A1 Pacific No. 60136 *Alcazar* of Doncaster on 17 June 1961. It was here in the early hours of 28 February 2021 a disastrous crash occurred when an Up HST crashed into a vehicle, which had come off the M62 motorway causing the HST to derail into the path of a freight train coming north resulting in ten deaths and numerous injuries.

Displaced from regular express passenger duties, Kings Cross A3 Pacific No. 60039 *Sandwich* has just crossed the swing bridge over the River Ouse at Selby with an Up express freight on Thursday 13 December 1962.

Having just been stopped at signals on the approach to the station at Selby, Thompson B1 4-6-0 No. 61306 is accelerating towards the swing bridge with its train of empty bogie wagons on 13 December 1962. At the time it was shedded at Hull Dairycoates, but it was subsequently moved to Low Moor, from where it was withdrawn in September 1967, but fortunately now preserved. I recall 13 December 1962 as my first trip out on a recently acquired second-hand Vespa scooter, hardly ideal weather with snow on the ground and one leg in plaster following a cartilage knee operation.

New England class 9F 2-10-0 No. 92142 is accelerating an Up train of empty mineral wagons from underneath the Great North Road on the approach to Doncaster station on Saturday 4 April 1964. Built in 1957, it was to have a ridiculously short life of less than ten years before being withdrawn from New England in March 1965 having spent its entire life shedded there.

How the mighty have fallen. In poor external condition and reduced to menial freight duties, Gresley A3 Pacific No. 60054 *Prince of Wales* is restarting a Down freight after suffering a signal check just north of Doncaster station on Saturday 4 April 1964. It had spent many years working expresses on both the East Coast main line and also the Great Central, but in October 1963 was moved to New England to where several more Pacifics had been moved when Kings Cross shed closed to steam in June 1963.

Wakefield class 4F 0-6-0 No. 44457 is struggling up the 1 in 55 gradient out of Dewsbury towards Earlsheaton on 29 March 1962 with a freight of mainly coal heading for Wrenthorpe Yard at Wakefield. It is on the ex-GNR line from Bradford to Wakefield via Dudley Hill and Ossett, which closed to passenger services in 1964. The majority of the track bed is now buried beneath industrial and residential development.

On Thursday 23 May 1963 Farnley Junction Jubilee class 4-6-0 No. 45695 *Minotaur* is restarting a local parcels train from Batley on its way from Leeds to Huddersfield. The platform of the former GNR station, which closed in September 1964, can be seen on the right.

3M30 Heaton to Manchester Red Bank empty newspaper vans was generally guaranteed to produce an interesting locomotive pairing from York, and on 23 May 1963 is drifting downhill from Morley Tunnel on the approach to Batley behind York class B1 4-6-0 No. 61062 and Newton Heath 'Crab' 2-6-0 No. 42750. The ex-GNR line is on the right climbing towards Drighlington & Adwalton.

The Standedge route across the Pennines carried not only a large number of passenger trains between Yorkshire and Lancashire, but also a huge amount of freight, particularly coal. On Wednesday 13 May 1964 Mirfield class WD 2-8-0 No. 90655 is heading an empty coal train returning from Lancashire to Healey Mills. It is drifting down the 1 in 105 gradient near Slaithwaite after emerging from the 3-mile 64-yard Standedge Tunnel at Marsden.

In December 1964, while I was working in Dewsbury, a Liverpool–Newcastle express is accelerating through Dewsbury Wellington Road station for the climb up to Morley Tunnel behind a Stanier class 5 4-6-0 and a BR Standard class 5 4-6-0, but unfortunately I didn't record the numbers of either.

On Saturday 28 October 1967 the Manchester Rail Travel Society and Severn Valley Railway Society jointly ran a special from Birmingham to parts of Lancashire and Yorkshire using several different locomotives. BR Standard class Britannia Pacific No. 70013 *Oliver Cromwell* was used on the section from Manchester Victoria to Normanton via Sheffield Victoria and is curving away from the Standedge route at Springwood Junction just outside Huddersfield on the way to Penistone and Sheffield.

A busy scene at Manchester Exchange on Saturday 18 August 1962 as Stanier class 4 2-6-4T No. 42442 of Patricroft sets off banking the 11.30 a.m. to Newcastle up the infamous Miles Platting bank of about 1.5 miles, partly at 1 in 47.

On Saturday 4 September 1955 the 'Northern Dales Rail Tour' was run jointly by the Stephenson Locomotive Society and the Manchester Locomotive Society using five different locomotives. Nicely turned out LMS Compound 4-4-0 No. 41102 of Blackpool is preparing to leave Manchester Victoria on the first leg of the tour, which it took to Tebay via Ingleton and Low Gill. (Fergus Johnson/John Whiteley collection)

Bypassing Manchester Exchange, Newton Heath Jubilee 4-6-0 No. 45652 *Hawke* is heading the Saturday 10.18 a.m. Manchester Victoria–Southport on 18 August 1962.

Hughes/Fowler Crab 2-6-0 No. 42758 of Gorton is accelerating the 11.45 a.m. Manchester Victoria–Southport through Exchange station on 18 August 1962, passing several onlookers and Patricroft BR Standard class 5 4-6-0 No. 73132 in the bay awaiting its next turn. Manchester Exchange was closed in 1969 when services were diverted to Victoria, but previously the two stations had shared the longest platform in Britain.

A holiday relief to Blackpool has just left Manchester Victoria behind Agecroft Jubilee 4-6-0 No. 45590 *Travancore*, with No. 42442 awaiting its next banking turn to Miles Platting. It is approaching Deal Street Junction on its way to Bolton, Preston and Blackpool and in the distance is the imposing building of Threlfalls Brewery.

On Sunday 21 July 1968 the Roch Valley Railway Society ran a special from Manchester Victoria to Southport and around other parts of Lancashire. Before the days of stringent health and safety legislation numerous onlookers and photographers are trackside as Lostock Hall Black Five No. 44888 passes Patricroft shed, which had closed a few weeks earlier.

Several rail tours were run on Sunday 4 August 1968 to mark the end of BR steam. Two nicely turned out Carnforth Black Five 4-6-0s, Nos. 44871 and 44894, are standing at Manchester Victoria prior to hauling the 'Farewell to Steam No. 1' organised by the Stephenson Locomotive Society (Midland), scheduled to leave at 11.20 a.m. The special originated at Birmingham and Nos. 44871 and 44894 headed the steam section of the tour from Manchester to Huddersfield, Blackburn, Rainhill and Stockport.

The Stephenson Locomotive Society and Manchester Locomotive Society jointly ran the 'West Cumberland Rail Tour' on Sunday 5 September 1954. The tour originated in Manchester and two separate Aspinall L&YR class 3F 0-6-0s were used on former Furness and L&NWR lines. No. 52501 worked the first steam section from Sellafield to Moor Row and Workington and is taking water having arrived at Workington Main. (Fergus Johnson/John Whiteley collection)

Another tour run jointly by the Stephenson Locomotive Society and the Manchester Locomotive Society was the 'Ashington Rail Tour' from Huddersfield on Saturday 10 June 1967 to the colliery and colliery lines at Ashington. Holbeck Jubilee No. 45562 *Alberta* worked the train from York to Ashington and back to York, and in the late afternoon is preparing to leave Ashington at 5.15 p.m. on the return, adjacent to the colliery line and platform.

Shortly after leaving Ashington, *Alberta* is passing North Seaton station, which had closed in November 1964, with some locals giving a cheery wave to the crew.

After stopping briefly at Newcastle, *Alberta* is passing King Edward Bridge Junction, having just crossed the River Tyne.

On Sunday 2 September 1956 the 'Tees-Tyne Rail Tour' originated at Manchester Victoria and ran to Darlington where various ex-NER lines were covered, several of which are now closed. Raven class B16 4-6-0 No. 61443 has just arrived at Bishop Auckland and passengers are returning to the train for the next section to Hartlepool after reversing. (Fergus Johnson/John Whiteley collection)

The RCTS and Stephenson Locomotive Society jointly ran 'The Wansbeck Wanderer' tour on Saturday 9 November 1963 on mainly ex-NB lines in Northumberland, many of which are now closed. It was mainly worked by well turned out Ivatt class 4 2-6-0 No. 43129 of Darlington, and while returning from Reedsmouth to Morpeth and Newcastle via the branch to Rothbury, it is pausing briefly at Woodburn, which had closed to passenger traffic in September 1952. The line closed completely in October 1966.

Having climbed to Grayrigg, unrebuilt Patriot class 4-6-0 No. 45501 *St. Dunstan's* of Carlisle Upperby is having a breather as it comes north through the Lune Gorge before taking on the mainly 1 in 75 climb to Shap Summit. It is heading a Down fitted freight on Tuesday 23 May 1961.

Dillicar water troughs were about 1 mile south of Tebay, and on Good Friday 12 April 1963 a morning Crewe–Carlisle parcels including some empty milk tanks is headed by Fairburn 2-6-4T No. 42110 of Tebay and Royal Scot 4-6-0 No. 46162 *Queen's Westminster Rifleman* of Upperby. Tebay shed was closed on Good Friday so instead of providing bankers for the climb to Shap Summit a pilot engine was attached at Oxenholme.

Britannia Pacific No. 70044 *Earl Haigh* of Crewe North is picking up water on the troughs as it speeds south on the morning Glasgow and Edinburgh–Birmingham on Good Friday 1963. The River Lune is just visible at a lower level and the M6 motorway now runs directly adjacent to the line here.

On several occasions I got soaked from an overfilled tender while at the side of the line, but fortunately on this occasion I was well away standing in the field as Kingmoor Black Five 4-6-0 No. 45293 rushed south with an Up fitted freight with the fireman slow to pick up the scoop.

Duchess Pacific No. 46238 *City of Carlisle* was generally always well turned out by Upperby. On summer bank holiday Monday 3 August 1964 it is picking up from the troughs while working the morning Crewe–Carlisle parcels with only a few more weeks left in service before being withdrawn on 12 September 1964.

Stanier class 8F 2-8-0 No. 48730 of Rose Grove is nearing its home shed as it passes Rose Grove West Junction heading the 08.35 Wyre Dock–Healey Mills coal empties on Tuesday 7 May 1968. It is crossing the Leeds-Liverpool Canal and Padiham Power Station, which was reached from Rose Grove West Junction, can just be seen in the distance.

The line from Hall Royd Junction, just east of Todmorden, to Gannow Junction at Burnley over Copy Pit saw a considerable amount of coal traffic from Yorkshire. The steep westbound climb is mainly at 1 in 65 and on Saturday 18 May 1968 Rose Grove 8F No. 48410 is being banked by another Rose Grove 8F as they near Copy Pit Summit with a heavy coal train from Healey Mills.

On Saturday 30 March 1968 Rose Grove Black Five No. 44899 is crossing the River Darwen after passing Pleasington heading the Darwen–Heysham oil tanks. The driver appears to be preparing for a short steep uphill climb before dropping down Hoghton Bank towards Lostock Hall.

As Gresley class K4 2-6-0 No. 61994 *The Great Marquess*, it was withdrawn from Dunfermline in December 1961, but was subsequently purchased by Viscount Garnock, returned to LNER apple green livery and worked several specials on the main line. On Sunday 16 April 1967 Epsom Railway Society ran 'The Mercian' tour, which originated at Euston. *The Great Marquess* worked the steam leg from Stockport Edgeley to Leeds Central and is near Rishton. At Leeds Central *Flying Scotsman* took over for the return to Kings Cross.

On Saturday 20 April 1968 the 'North West Tour' was run using several different locomotives on a circuitous journey around parts of Lancashire and Yorkshire. BR Standard class 5 4-6-0s Nos 73134 and 73069 worked the special from Stalybridge to Bolton via Standedge and Copy Pit, and at 12.48 are departing from Stalybridge.

On the penultimate weekend of BR steam, Black Five 4-6-0s Nos 45073 and 45156 (formerly *Ayrshire Yeomanry*) are leaving Blackburn on Sunday 28 July 1968 with the 'Farewell to BR Steam Rail Tour' from Birmingham, which used six different steam locomotives on a route around Lancashire and Yorkshire. At 12.48 they are leaving on the Skipton–Rose Grove section of the tour.

On Saturday 6 April 1968 Rose Grove 8F 2-8-0 No. 48448 has just burst out of Towneley Tunnel after passing Gannow Junction at Burnley. It is climbing the 1 in 68 to Copy Pit while heading the Wyre Dock–Healey Mills coal empties.

Almost down to walking pace, No. 48448 has just emerged from Holme Tunnel and is on the last few hundred yards of the climb with the Wyre Dock–Healey Mills coal empties on 6 April 1968.

At Hall Royd Junction, Todmorden, No. 48448 joined the Calder Valley main line from Manchester and is on easy downhill grades all the way to Healey Mills. With only about 6 miles to Healey Mills, it is passing Heaton Lodge Junction near Mirfield with the L&NWR New Line to Leeds visible on the right.

With only a few weeks left in service, Carnforth class 9F 2-10-0 No. 92160 is drifting downhill towards Clapham on the Little North Western line heading a loaded coal train from Leeds to Carnforth on Saturday 8 June 1968. Having been built at Crewe in November 1957, No. 92160 was one of the last 9Fs to be withdrawn, on 29 June 1968, a ridiculously short life of less than eleven years.

Initially Midland Shed No. 28, later changed to 20A and becoming 55A when Leeds Holbeck, depot was transferred to the North Eastern Region of British Rail, it incorporated a large roundhouse with two turntables, which could accommodate forty-four locomotives. On Sunday 16 April 1961 inside the shed is long-term resident of Holbeck class 8F 2-8-0 No. 48399, with Jubilee class 4-6-0 No. 45677 *Beatty* visiting from Glasgow Corkerhill.

A view of the shed yard at Holbeck taken from the twin coal hopper on Sunday 17 March 1963, with the main line to Sheffield just visible on the right and the ex-L&NWR Viaduct line to Farnley Junction and Huddersfield in the background.

Inside Holbeck roundhouse on 28 July 1967. Facing one of the turntables, from left to right, are Ivatt class 4 2-6-0 No. 43076, Black Five 4-6-0 No. 45156 (formerly *Ayrshire Yeomanry*), Jubilee 4-6-0 No. 45593 *Kolhapur* and Black Five 4-6-0 No. 45428, all at home apart from No. 45156, which was visiting from Edge Hill.

Copley Hill shed at Leeds was smaller than Holbeck, shed code 37B in the Eastern Region, but becoming 56C in 1956 in the North Eastern Region. It was a five road straight shed, but played host to the glamorous LNER Pacifics until closure in 1964. On Tuesday 19 March 1963, when I should have been at college, Kings Cross A4 Pacific No. 60008 *Dwight D. Eisenhower* is at the west end of the shed alongside Copley Hill B1 4-6-0 No. 61016 *Inyala*.

Standing in the shed yard at Holbeck on Sunday 16 April 1961 is long-term resident Royal Scot 4-6-0 No. 46117 *Welsh Guardsman*, behind which is BR Standard class 5 4-6-0 No. 73171, also of Holbeck. In the background are class 9F 2-10-0 No. 92050 of Rowsley, class 9F 2-10-0 No. 92157 of Saltley and another long-term resident of Holbeck, Jubilee class 4-6-0 No. 45605 *Cyprus*.

A picture taken from Nineveh Road bridge at Holbeck on Tuesday 21 May 1963 sees Stourton class 4F 0-6-0 No. 43987 passing Engine Shed Junction with empties off the Aire Valley line heading for Stourton. The busy yard at Holbeck shed is on the left dominated by the large twin coaling tower.

Skipton 4F 0-6-0 No. 44125 is passing beneath Nineveh Road bridge and the entrance to Leeds Holbeck shed as it struggles to restart a coal train from Stourton to the Aire Valley line on Tuesday 5 March 1963.

Originally NER/LNWR Leeds New station, later Leeds City South, York class V2 2-6-2 No. 60907 is preparing to leave the east end of platform eleven with the Sunday 2.45 p.m. to Newcastle on 1 April 1962. The once magnificent roof of this vast station is in the process of being demolished prior to redevelopment.

Later in the afternoon of Sunday 1 April 1962, unrebuilt Patriot class 4-6-0 No. 45507 *Royal Tank Corps* of Lancaster is preparing to leave the Wellington side, Leeds City North, with a train for Carnforth and Morecambe, having just attached a van. The Queens Hotel is dominant in the background. In early 1962 some of the last remaining unrebuilt Patriots had been transferred to Lancaster to help out on the Morecambe–Leeds and Bradford trains, but within months they had all been withdrawn.

On the morning of Tuesday 19 February 1963 Farnley Junction Jubilee class 4-6-0 No. 45695 *Minotaur* is passing Leeds City Junction having just left Leeds City South with the 8.45 a.m. Newcastle–Liverpool. It is taking the ex-L&NWR Viaduct line as a Black Five from an earlier arrival makes its way round to Holbeck shed for servicing.

In 1960 eight Gresley class A3 Pacifics were transferred to Leeds Holbeck to work expresses over the demanding Settle and Carlisle route, replacing the ageing Royal Scots, although most of the A3s were transferred away by July 1961. On Sunday 19 February 1961 No. 60082 *Neil Gow* is passing Leeds City Junction with the Down 'Thames-Clyde Express', having arrived at Holbeck from Heaton in May 1960. It was transferred back to Heaton in July 1961 before being withdrawn from Gateshead in September 1963.

Also on Sunday 19 February 1961 Gresley class A3 Pacific No. 60088 *Book Law* is rounding the sharp corner from Whitehall Junction as it approaches Leeds City North with the Up 'Thames-Clyde Express'. *Book Law* had also been transferred to Holbeck from Heaton, and was to return there in July 1961 when the onset of dieselisation was displacing the A3s from the majority of regular main line duties.

Unrebuilt Patriot 4-6-0 No. 45507 *Royal Tank Corps* restarting a train from Morecambe and Carnforth to Leeds City, having been stopped at signals at Leeds City Junction on Saturday 31 March 1962.

An interesting pairing of locomotives heading the Heaton–Manchester Red Bank empty newspaper vans on Saturday 11 April 1964. Kingmoor Britannia Pacific No. 70009 *Alfred the Great* is piloting BR Standard class 4 4-6-0 No. 75043 of Aintree on the climb away from Leeds City Junction to Farnley Junction on the Viaduct line, which was abandoned in the 1980s.

Farnley Junction class WD 2-8-0 No. 90503 is passing its home shed on Tuesday 28 May 1963 with a train of empty coaching stock to Manchester. It is on the long climb of almost 5 miles from Leeds City Junction to Morley Tunnel. The ex-L&NWR New Line to Heaton Lodge Junction at Mirfield can be seen above the coaches.

Royal Scot class 4-6-0 No. 46105 *Cameron Highlander* of Polmadie is accelerating a Down fitted freight past Whitehall Junction on Saturday 3 February 1962. The line diverging to the right is the original L&NWR line to Huddersfield via Morley.

On Tuesday 18 December 1962 Stourton class 4F 0-6-0 No. 44335 is passing Wortley Junction with a Down coal train heading towards Shipley and from there either to Bradford or Skipton. It has just passed the remains of Holbeck Low Level station, which had closed in 1958, and on the right are Wortley gas sidings.

A view from the steps of Wortley Junction signal box as Holbeck Black Five 4-6-0 No. 44828 passes on Saturday 5 November 1966 with a Stourton–Carlisle freight as a diesel shunts wagons in the gas sidings.

Taken from inside Wortley Junction signal box looking north on Saturday 25 May 1963, Normanton class 8F 2-8-0 No. 48084 is passing on coal empties. The entrance to the gas works is on the left, Wortley NE signal box on the right and Kirkstall Power Station in the far distance.

On Saturday 18 April 1964 Kingmoor Black Five 4-6-0 No. 44887 is leaving Bradford Forster Square with the 4.40 p.m. stopper to Carlisle. The extensive carriage sidings are on the right, part of which were to form the site of the much smaller new Forster Square station, which was opened in 1990, and on the left is Valley Road goods yard.

The afternoon vans to Heysham is leaving Bradford Forster Square on Wednesday 15 March 1967 behind one of Holbeck's last Jubilees, No. 45593, formerly named *Kolhapur*, the nameplates having been removed for safekeeping. Earlier in the afternoon the train had been brought from Leeds by Britannia Pacific No. 70038 *Robin Hood*, which would later take the 4.30 p.m. to Birmingham as far as Leeds.

I regularly photographed the afternoon vans to Heysham during 1967 while I was working at the District Valuer's office in Bradford, which could coincide with some outside valuation work! Grubby Holbeck Black Five No. 44857 has just left Forster Square and is passing the turntable, which has just been used by Britannia Pacific No. 70034 *Thomas Hardy* to turn after bringing the vans from Leeds.

On an early May evening in 1967 Stanier 2-6-4T No. 42665 of Low Moor is preparing to leave Forster Square on a parcels train that it will work as far as Leeds. At the time considerable parcels traffic was generated by Bradford's Grattan and Empire Stores, which sadly disappeared in the late 1970s as it was switched to road transport. Having spent considerable time at Tebay as a Shap banker, it had been transferred to Low Moor a few weeks earlier, but was withdrawn at the end of June 1967.

On an evening in March 1967, Britannia Pacific No. 70048, formerly named *The Territorial Army 1908–1958*, of Carlisle Kingmoor, is waiting to leave Valley Road Goods at Bradford on the 7.45 p.m. freight to Carlisle. This once busy goods yard declined during the 1970s, was closed in 1984 and subsequently developed as a large retail park.

Stanier 2-6-4T No. 42616 of Low Moor is leaving the ex-L&YR and GNR terminus at Bradford Exchange on Sunday 30 July 1967 with the 2.18 p.m. to Leeds, which will then continue to London Kings Cross. The former L&YR signal box that controlled the station is on the left, but Exchange station would soon be replaced by a new combined rail and bus station, which opened in 1973 as Bradford Interchange.

The two summer Saturday 8.20 a.m. departures from Bradford Exchange, one to Bridlington and one to Skegness, nicely positioned following requests from enthusiasts on 29 July 1967. On the left is Low Moor Black Five No. 44694 with a Fairburn 2-6-4T banker climbing the 1 in 50 to Bowling Junction on the Bridlington train travelling via Halifax, and on the right Low Moor Black Five No. 44662 is starting the climb to Laisterdyke on the Skegness train via Leeds.

Once the pride of Stewarts Lane working prestige boat trains such as the 'Golden Arrow', Britannia Pacific No. 70004, formerly named *William Shakespeare,* is near Frizinghall shortly after leaving Bradford Valley Road Goods with the 7.45 p.m. freight to Carlisle in June 1967.

In March 1967 Wakefield class 9F 2-10-0 No. 92135 is coming slowly round the sharp curve at Shipley with its speed restriction of 20 mph heading a Stourton–Carlisle freight. It is approaching Shipley Bingley Junction where platforms on the Leeds–Skipton line were later built, and the station car park was formed on land to the right in the centre of the triangle of lines.

With Shipley Bingley Junction signal box on the left, Kingmoor Black Five 4-6-0 No. 44903 drifts slowly around Shipley Curve with a Morecambe and Carnforth–Leeds train on Tuesday 26 March 1963. This was one of three signal boxes operating the triangle of lines at Shipley, all of which were decommissioned in 1994 when the lines were electrified.

Hughes/Fowler Crab 2-6-0 No. 42905 of Carlisle Kingmoor is accelerating a northbound coal train away from Shipley Bingley Junction on Tuesday 26 March 1963.

On Saturday 27 May 1961, long-time Holbeck Royal Scot class 4-6-0 No. 46113 *Cameronian* has just passed Bingley heading the up 'Waverley' towards Leeds City North, where the train will reverse and another locomotive will come on to take it south on its journey to St Pancras.

Midland Railway Fowler class 4F 0-6-0 No. 43968 of Stourton with right-hand drive is trundling north as it nears Bingley with a coal train bound for Keighley and Skipton on 27 May 1961. Having been built in 1922, it was to survive until late in 1965 when it was withdrawn from Royston.

Towards the end of March 1967 Holbeck Black Five 4-6-0 No. 44828 is leaving Skipton with the 2.53 p.m. Leeds–Heysham vans, which it has worked from Bradford Forster Square. On the right is the disused platform on the line to Grassington, which opened in 1902 but closed to regular passenger traffic in 1930. However, part of the line remains open to this day for stone traffic from the quarry at Rylstone, the section to Grassington having been completely closed in 1969 and subsequently lifted.

An unidentified class 9F 2-10-0 with neither a shed code nor smokebox number is rolling into Skipton past Skipton Station South signal box in June 1967 with the Haverton Hill–Heysham tanks.

On Saturday 18 May 1968 one of the remaining BR Standard class 4 4-6-os, No. 75019, is preparing to leave Spencer's Lime Works at Swinden End near Rylstone with a train of ballast.

No. 75019 was a regular performer on the stone trains on the former Grassington Branch in the last few months of BR steam, and on Friday 31 May 1968 it is struggling away from Swinden End with a heavy train of ballast on its journey down the branch to the main line at Skipton. The works are in the background, which are now bypassed by a new road on the right of this picture.

Two of the last few Jubilees to remain in service are at Skipton North in the early evening of Monday 19 June 1967. No. 45675, formerly named *Hardy*, is being inspected by the driver as it stands adjacent to the shed on the 7.45 p.m. freight from Bradford Valley Road to Carlisle as No. 45562, formerly named *Alberta*, rushes past with the lightweight Heysham vans.

In 1967 the summer Saturday reliefs over the Settle and Carlisle line were diagrammed to the remaining Holbeck Jubilees, and on 12 August 1967 No. 45593, formerly named *Kolhapur*, is nearing Gargrave heading the relief to the Down 'Thames-Clyde Express'.

On Sunday 28 July 1968 the two remaining BR Standard class 4 4-6-0s Nos 75019 and 75027 are heading the Carnforth–Skipton section of the 'Farewell to BR Steam Rail Tour' having just passed Hellifield.

Work-stained class 8F 2-8-0 No. 48318 of Carlisle Kingmoor is restarting from a signal check adjacent to Hellifield shed heading a Carlisle–Stourton freight on Tuesday 31 March 1964.

Carnforth class 9F 2-10-0 No. 92160 is nearing its withdrawal date at the end of June 1968, but on Saturday 8 June 1968 is heading a rake of thirty-one loaded coal wagons from Stourton to Carnforth. Fortuitously I saw it passing Keighley, and with relatively quiet roads in those days, managed to get numerous photographs of it between there and Clapham. In the early afternoon it is taking the Carnforth line at Settle Junction much to the amusement of the driver and fireman.

Kingmoor Black Five 4-6-0 No. 45254 is approaching Ais Gill Summit, highest point on the magnificent Settle and Carlisle line at 1,169 feet above sea level. Overlooked by Wild Boar Fell, it is heading a Carlisle–Stourton freight of mainly coal empties on Saturday 30 April 1966 climbing the last section of 1 in 100 near the top of an unbroken climb of about 15 miles from Ormside Viaduct, just south of Appleby.

A stranger on the Settle and Carlisle line in the form of Castle class 4-6-0 No. 7029 *Clun Castle*, which is battling against the 1 in 100 gradient and a strong westerly wind on the approach to Blea Moor on Saturday 30 September 1967. It is working the 'Splendour of Steam Rail Tour' organised by the A4 Preservation Society on the Peterborough–Carlisle leg, the return train hauled by No. 4498 *Sir Nigel Gresley*. Having been withdrawn in December 1965, *Clun Castle* was purchased by Patrick Whitehouse in 1966 and based at Tyseley.

On the bitterly cold and frosty morning of Thursday 7 December 1967, Kingmoor Britannia Pacific No. 70045, formerly named *Lord Rowallan*, is at Helm, about 3 miles south of Appleby, digging in for the long climb to Ais Gill with the 8.05 a.m. Carlisle–Red Bank empty vans, which was diverted from the West Coast main line due to problems at Penrith.

Princess Coronation Pacifics were rarely seen on the Settle and Carlisle line, but on Sunday 12 July 1964 No. 46255 *City of Hereford* of Carlisle Kingmoor is nearing Ais Gill Summit heading the return 'Pacific Pennine Rail Tour' organised by the Stephenson Locomotive Society. The tour ran from Birmingham New Street to Carlisle and *City of Hereford* worked it back from Carlisle to Leeds.

Saturday 4 November 1967 was a clear, frosty morning on the Settle and Carlisle line as Heaton Mersey class 8F 2-8-0 No. 48074 emerged from Blea Moor Tunnel heading a Down freight for Carlisle.

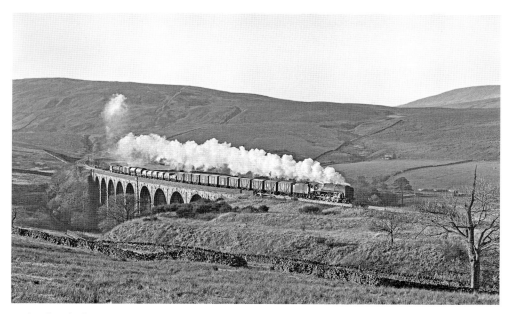

Birkenhead class 9F 2-10-0 No. 92082 has also just emerged from Blea Moor Tunnel on 4 November 1967 and is crossing Dent Head Viaduct with a Down freight. Having climbed to Blea Moor, it is now on the easy grades past Dent and Garsdale to Ais Gill Summit before the predominantly downhill run of about 50 miles to Carlisle.

On Saturday 6 May 1967 Kingmoor class 9F 2-10-0 No. 92249 has just passed Horton-in-Ribblesdale heading the Widnes–Long Meg empty anhydrite hoppers. No. 92249 was one of the last 9Fs to be built, at the end of 1958, and was fitted with a double chimney. It was destined to have a ridiculously short life of less than ten years, as it was withdrawn from Speke Junction in May 1968.

Having climbed at 1 in 100 for about 5 miles, Kingmoor class 9F 2-10-0 No. 92125 is about to have a short breather on a small section of level track at Helwith Bridge before continuing to climb to Blea Moor on Saturday 15 July 1967 with a Stourton–Carlisle freight.

Newton Heath Black Five 4-6-0 No. 44803 is storming towards Birkett Tunnel in December 1967 with an Up freight from Carlisle.

Sunday 11 August 1968 will be etched into the memory of many railway enthusiasts as the last day of BR steam when BR ran 1T57 as the 'Last Steam Hauled Rail Tour', the 'Fifteen Guinea Special' as it became known. A Black Five hauled it from Liverpool Lime Street to Manchester Victoria where Britannia Pacific No. 70013 *Oliver Cromwell* took over for the run to Carlisle. At about 1.55 p.m., thirty-four minutes late, it is crossing Batty Moss Viaduct at Ribblehead on the way to Carlisle where it was due to arrive at 2.56 p.m.

The special left Carlisle on the return at about 3.45 p.m., fifteen minutes late, hauled by two Carnforth Black Five 4-6-0s, Nos 44871 and 44781, which took the train back to Manchester Victoria. Right on time at about 4.45 p.m., they are crossing Ais Gill Viaduct witnessed by scores of enthusiasts – all roads in the area were completely gridlocked.

Weather in the Peak District in early February 1968 produced a good covering of snow accompanied by blue skies. On Saturday 3 February class 8F 2-8-0 No. 48117 of Heaton Mersey is down to walking pace as it struggles into Buxton with a freight from Gowhole Yard in its last few weeks of existence. It was withdrawn on 23 March 1968.

Also on 3 February 1968, Buxton 8F No. 48442 has just set back near the remains of Chapel-en-le-Frith Central station, which had closed on 6 March 1967. It has restarted wrong line due to engineering work in Dove Holes Tunnel on the steep climb at 1 in 90 to Peak Forest and is heading a freight from Gowhole Yard.

Having worked wrong line through Dove Holes Tunnel on Thursday 15 February 1968, Buxton class 8F 2-8-0 No. 48532 is crossing over at Peak Forest with a freight for Buxton, which also includes some wagons for ICI Tunstead at Great Rocks Junction.

Since my first visit to Shap in the spring of 1961 it has had a magnetic attraction, particularly the south slope with its climb of about 5 miles from Tebay at mainly 1 in 75 to Shap Summit. On Saturday 17 July 1965 Polmadie BR Standard class 5 4-6-0 No. 73060 has just come over the summit with an Up relief and the fireman can now enjoy the downhill run to Tebay.

Later in the afternoon of 17 July 1965 Kingmoor Britannia Pacific No. 70041, formerly named *Sir John Moore*, suffered a cruel signal check at Salterwath approaching Shap Wells while heading the thirteen-coach 1.05 p.m. Manchester–Glasgow and Edinburgh including a Liverpool portion. Expertly handled by the crew, seemingly in good mechanical condition and with a full head of steam, it made a sure-footed start on the final 1 in 75 to the summit.

Blackpool Jubilee class 4-6-0 No. 45574 *India* is just about to pass Scout Green signal box heading the Sunday 11.00 a.m. Euston–Carlisle on 19 July 1964.

Dumfries Black Five 4-6-0 No. 45432 has probably been attached as pilot to get it home as Willesden Britannia Pacific No. 70015 *Apollo* would be sufficient power to work the 4.15 p.m. Manchester–Glasgow on spring bank holiday Monday 22 May 1961. The pair are storming north between Greenholme and Scout Green.

One of my favourite positions on the section from Tebay to Shap Summit was at the approach to the cutting near the summit where the delightful open landscape of the Westmorland Fells can be seen, later to become part of Cumbria. The Sunday 1.05 p.m. Manchester–Glasgow and Edinburgh including a Liverpool portion was first seen almost 3 miles away at Greenholme. Several minutes later it is approaching the summit cutting with Fairburn 2-6-4T of Carnforth piloting Rose Grove Black Five No. 45218 on 28 June 1964.

In deplorable external condition, Crewe North Duchess Pacific No. 46228 *Duchess of Rutland* is passing Shap Wells with the 10.30 a.m. Euston–Carlisle on Saturday 25 July 1964 in its last few weeks of service. It was withdrawn early in September 1964.

Good Friday 12 April 1963 was a day of sunshine and sleet showers on the fells with a strong westerly wind. Fortunately in a sunny period, nicely turned out Upperby Duchess Pacific No. 46225 *Duchess of Gloucester* came storming round the corner at Greenholme heading 1S63, a Euston–Glasgow relief.

Coming effortlessly up the 1 in 75 towards the summit cutting on Sunday 12 July 1964, Crewe North Duchess Pacific No. 46251 *City of Nottingham* is heading the 'Pacific Pennine Rail Tour' from Birmingham to Carlisle organised by the Stephenson Locomotive Society.

On Sunday 28 June 1964 Tebay shed was closed and any Down train needing assistance would take on a pilot at Oxenholme instead of a banker at Tebay. Fairburn 2-6-4T No. 42198 of Carnforth is piloting Newton Heath Black Five 4-6-0 No. 44676, which is fitted with a self-weighing tender as the pair storm past Scout Green on a Crewe–Carlisle parcels.

In its final few weeks of service, Carlisle Upperby Duchess Pacific No. 46250 *City of Lichfield* is still working one of the West Coast premier trains. It is racing past Shap Wells heading the Sunday Down 'Midday Scot' on 19 July 1964.

With a dusting of snow on the ground, I was grateful of a hot cup of tea and a chat with the signalman in his tiny box at Scout Green on Saturday 3 December 1966. Kingmoor class 9F 2-10-0 No. 92076 is approaching the level crossing, with a Tebay 2-6-4T banker working equally hard at the rear.

Kingmoor class 9F 2-10-0 No. 92004 is storming past Greenholme on 4 November 1967 with a Down train of oil tanks. Out of sight banking assistance is being provided by one of Tebay's BR Standard class 4 4-6-0s, which had recently replaced the 2-6-4Ts that had long been associated with Tebay.

On Saturday 7 October 1967 Lostock Hall Black Five 4-6-0 No. 45444 is climbing slowly past Shap Wells with a Down freight for Carlisle including some empty cattle wagons towards the front. Banking assistance is being provided by BR Standard class 4 4-6-0 No. 75037, which had been moved to Tebay in May 1967 to eek out the last few months of its life.

Late in the afternoon of Saturday 27 June 1964, Rose Grove WD 2-8-0 No. 90181 draws slowly forward at Tebay, having just whistled for a banker for the climb to Shap Summit on a heavy Down freight. The banker is just about to come off shed on the right-hand side in the shape of a Fairburn 2-6-4T, and in the distance are wagons on part of the ex-NER line to Kirkby Stephen and Darlington, which had closed in 1962.

On Saturday 7 October 1967 BR Standard class 4 4-6-0 No.75037 is banking a heavy northbound freight on the 1 in 75 climb to Shap Summit, having been moved to Tebay for banking duties from Stoke earlier in 1967.